Want *free* info about Getting Laid?

- – Get a *free* email newsletter about getting laid
- – Get tips and seduction techniques
- – Get your seduction questions answered

All this is at **http://howtosucceedwithwomen.com**
Or email **info@howtosucceedwithwomen.com**

THE RULES FOR GETTING LAID

David Graff
&
Ray Schwartz

For information, contact:
Drill Press
PO Box 55094
Madison, WI 53705-8894

ISBN 0-9613177-5-2

Printed in Canada

10   9   8   7   6   5

DISCLAIMER

Neither the authors nor the publisher of this book are responsible for the use or misuse of the ideas and information presented. The reader is warned that the information contained is highly controversial.

The book is presented for entertainment uses only. Be warned that this book does not assert the legality of any of the methods it describes. The authors disclaim any responsibility for damages resulting from using or for misusing the methods or the consequences of implementing anything contained herein.

Please note, any sexual interactions with women *must* be consensual. The authors and publisher encourage men to be careful and to make sure they have consent for *all* sexual interactions.

INTRODUCTION
BY KAREN KRIZANOVICH

W hat's the hardest thing about *The Rules For Getting Laid*? Keeping the book in your possession. Although as a woman I shouldn't have access to this brilliant reservoir of male sexual expertise, *The Rules For Getting Laid* has proven itself to be the book every man wants to read. To own. To pore over. To steal. This is the kind of book men have probably slept with me to get. I wish I'd bought more copies. Perhaps then I would have one left for reference for myself?

The Rules For Getting Laid is the strong arm of forbidden knowledge in an otherwise limp-wristed, needlessly dull and over-cautious world of sex books. The value of *The Rules* is that it isn't slick, pristine or polite. It is, dare I say, a slim yet manly tome of exactly what's going on in men's minds: what they want and what women look like to them from inside. Reading *The Rules* is like waking up one morning and discovering that you are a sexually-focused man. Thank God its authors tell you sure-fire ways to become a sexually-satisfied man. This book tells the reader what it is like to tangle with the overpowering, puzzling and actually rather pleasant beast of heterosexual sex—without once making it shameful or unworthy.

The authors are men who love sex and love women: luckily, they are also writers gifted in modern parlance. When other sex books waver interminably, every chapter of *The Rules* puts practicality and clarity first. When it comes to understanding women, presenting yourself as a lover and being the best man you can be in bed, this is not merely a book: this is the User's Manual with which every man should have been born.

If it sounds as if I like *The Rules To Getting Laid*, be certain that I do. Mostly, however, for the insight it gives to everyone—men and women—on what men want, how they think and how everybody can be happier, even when vertical.

The Rules For Getting Laid should be outlawed: with books like this, women don't stand a chance of *not* having great sex. *The Rules For Getting Laid* is the best book I've ever read on how to treat women—it's the *Black Beauty* of the female world. *The Rules For Getting Laid* contains enough cunning information to give any man the magnetism of Cary Grant and the success rate of Casanova—without leaving town!

A book like this is so good it makes me want to go out and seduce women too!

—Karen Krizanovich
  London, UK
  October 12, 1998

AUTHOR'S INTRODUCTION

This book was written to teach you the critical secrets about getting laid. The authors have learned the hard way. We made all the mistakes you can imagine. But four years ago we decided that, working together, we would master dating and getting laid. The masterpiece you hold in your hands is the result of our efforts.

Four years later, we both have abundant sex lives and the respect of many men. You can have this too if you read this book carefully and, more importantly, get out and flirt, talk, date, and interact with women. Getting laid is a skill like riding a bike. Once you learn how, it *will* be effortless. Stay focused on your goal, be patient, and this book will lead you to many nights of hot sex.

This book honestly and accurately outlines the work you must do to get a woman in bed. It is your Bible for knowing how to behave and what to do when in seduction situations. But let us give you a warning: because this book and the techniques in it are so interesting and so cool, you may be tempted to tell women about this book, or show it to them. *Don't do it.*

It's difficult to overestimate the catastrophic consequences of showing this book to a woman. If you confess to a woman that you are studying seduction she will be offended and not sleep with you, but the problem won't stop there. She will also tell your friends, and tell anyone you know that you have a seduction book and are trying to seduce women. She will poison your chances with any woman she tells, and everyone you know will humiliate you by asking you about it.

Only tell men you can trust about this book. (In case you don't know, a man you can trust is one whom you've told a secret to who hasn't told other people about it.) Tell them where to buy their own copy of this book (experience shows that if you loan them your copy, most men will keep it for up to a year). Discuss what you are doing with these trusty men. Just don't talk to women about it.

The amazing thing is, despite the warning we're giving here, some readers will think they are "above the law." They will talk about this book to women, and show them their copy of it. Or they buy our tape series, and play it for women. If you are one of these men, read the warnings above again, and when you want to talk to women about this book, talk about something else instead.

You have been warned. You will ultimately pay the price for being a moron!

A skill of every dating commando is the ability to be sneaky and crafty. In the monkey kingdom, the most sneaky monkeys get the most sex, not the alpha males, as you might assume. Studies show that while the alpha male is leading and disciplining monkeys who challenge his leadership, craftier monkeys are screwing every red-ass female monkey in sight. While the alpha male is sleeping, the sneaky crafty male is fucking his wife right in front of him, and she wants him, too. You must be like these crafty monkeys, and learn to create strategies to get women. This book will show you how.

THE 6 PROBLEMS INSIDE YOU

There is no shortage of single women to fuck. You must realize that the reason why you are not having lots of sex is because of you and your attitudes. We are not blaming you or even taunting you—yet. We know that no one taught you the secrets of getting laid. However, it will take a change in your attitude to become successful, and you must hold yourself accountable for making the necessary changes.

Here is a list of the problems many men fall into. Do you see yourself on it?

1. You believe that you are a "nice guy."

The fact of the matter is that you are a horny jerk just like the rest of us. Get over it!

2. You are a klutz who can't impress a woman.

Every man has within his grasp the power to bag a woman. Every man has charming aspects to his personality that are attractive to women. This book will show you how to find and capitalize on them.

3. You are waiting for a woman to meet you halfway.

Women are never going to meet you halfway. Dating isn't fair. Stop wishing it was different and get out there!

4. You don't know what to say to women.

Most of us blow it in conversations with women. So what? The most important key is just to keep going and talk anyway. This book will cover the basics of what to say and what not to say.

5. You are scared.

Admit it. You are just as wimpy as the next guy. Timidity and nervousness are the most common problems reported by our students. It is natural. By the end of the book you will increase your confidence level and become a more powerful motherfucker.

6. *You don't know where to go to meet women.*

This is another excuse we get from many men. We will show you how to spot dozens of places to meet and bag women.

SEX COSTS TOO MUCH!

James Baldwin said that "money, it turned out was exactly like sex—you thought of nothing else if you didn't have it and thought of other things if you did." Sex is the world's most expensive commodity. This book will show you how to never overpay.

Men's need for sex topples empires. However, you must be willing to set limits around how far you will go for sex. Most men go too far and end up paying too much for this commodity.

You don't yet realize it, but you've overpaid for sex in the past and will continue until you become a "Rules Man." Paying for sex usually takes the form of paying for dates and expending too much energy and time on getting a woman into bed. Many men even get married in hopes of having a steady supply of sex, and we all know of men who have lost their reputations by going after hookers and other women. Worst of all, when you overpay for sex, you lose your self-respect and the respect of other men.

Just look at how much a divorce costs: Let's say you end a five year marriage paying a woman $80,000 in the divorce settlement. Let's be generous and say you were having sex on average twice per week. You would have had sex 110 times in a year and 550 times over five years. Under those circumstances you would have ended up paying around $144.00 per fuck, with the same woman. That may not seem like a lot. But you end up wasting lots more time and usually spend more money, and never really get what you are after. Getting married just to get sex is a bad idea.

It's not worth hurting your self-respect to get sex. It isn't even worth bouncing a check to get sex. We are committed to creating a world where men have a steady supply of women at all times and do not overpay. Follow the Rules and join us in creating this world of sexual abundance.

Short Term-Relationships versus Long-Term

This book is about mastering short-term relationships. We define short-term relationships as ones where you fuck the woman 4–10 times and then get rid of her. Long term relationships are ones in which you are planning on being monogamous with the woman for years and years. This book will cover a few basic principles that will help you with long-term relationships, but its focus is on teaching you mastery of the short-term. It is our belief that you must master short term relationships before you can have a successful long term relationship. If a man dates a woman out of obligation, or because he feels he can't get someone better, he is stuck and will not be happy. It is only after a man realizes that he could have

18

several other women that he can decide on one
that will satisfy his requirements for a long-term
mate.

And now, **The Rules for Getting Laid**.

1. MAKE HER FEEL SPECIAL, AND SHE'LL GIVE YOU SEX

If you are like us, you've listened when women have told you that they wanted equality, and wanted to be treated the same way men are treated. What they didn't tell you, because they didn't know it, was that they want to be treated the way they *imagine* men are treated. In point of fact, many women labor under the delusion that men's lives are really easy and that anything a man wants is automatically handed to him, usually by a woman. As guys, we understand that life is rough and no one is going out of their way to protect us or make it easy for us. So when women told you they wanted equality and you said to yourself, "Okay, I'll treat you like any other guy," you probably noticed that when you did so, they didn't put out for you. The bottom line is that, no matter what a woman says, you have *got* to make her feel special if you want sex. You have got to do the work, find out what things make her feel like a princess in a fairy tale, and then do those things.

To seduce a woman, you must take her into another world, a special world where only the two of you exist, a romantic world, a poetic world. Sometimes this happens automatically with a woman: if you've ever fallen in love, you remember what it's like to feel like you are the only two people who've ever existed. You probably also remembered that, in that state, she really wanted sex. A lot. If you haven't ever felt that, don't despair—by following these simple guidelines, you can learn to *create* those special feelings. It's your responsibility, if you want to get laid. So how do you do it?

• Keep on the lookout for romantic ideas or situations. You can train your mind to always be looking for ways that little romantic moments can be created. The other day a friend of ours was at a Chinese restaurant, and got the fortune

"Take the next opportunity you see—it will be wonderful" in his fortune cookie. Seeing an attractive woman sitting alone, he wrote his name and phone number on the back of the fortune, and as he left stopped at her table and said "you look lonely here…perhaps this fortune will cheer you up. By the way, I think you look beautiful." She smiled and accepted the fortune and he smiled and left. Two days later she called him and they now have a date planned.

This effortless introduction worked because it created a small, special moment in her otherwise busy, stressful day. He was appreciating her. He was doing something romantic. You can tell if an idea is romantic by asking yourself, "would a woman look back on it as incredibly special?" Our friend knew that the fortune cookie was a tale a woman would gladly tell about how she met her boyfriend. So it was romantic, made her feel special, and it worked.

• Look like you put thought into it. Women feel special, just like anybody does, if they think someone has done some preparation just for them. Cooking a meal, wrapping a little present, or hand-making a card for her will all make her feel like you are sitting around thinking of ways to delight her. The key here is to do things that give the appearance that you are thinking of her, even if you are not. When you do things to make her feel special and appreciated it will increase her desire to put out for you.

• Do something special and "out of the ordinary." Don't take a woman to the same place you'd go with buddies if you want sex. Take her someplace out of the ordinary. A river front cafe in a nearby small town, a walk in the woods where you've previously and secretly stashed a bottle of champaign, two glasses and a blanket you can "discover" together are all examples of "out of the ordinary" events. Even art films (if she likes that kind of thing) or museums can be out-of-the-ordinary events. You can *be* an "out of the ordinary" man if you know some love poetry by heart. That will make her feel very special.

• Focus on the details. Women want the "little things," so you should make sure every little thing is right when you are seducing a woman. This means flowers, new candles just lit for the first time, clean linens, the works. Everything is clean, nothing is sloppy. Romance is in the details, and you must have them right in order to succeed.

Just as a businessman is always looking for new situations that can make money, a "man's man" is always looking for new situations that can create romantic feelings. If you take on this practice you'll make her feel special, and you will get laid.

2. SHOW YOUR ROMANTIC INTEREST RIGHT AWAY

D o you want to learn a good way to waste a lot of time seducing a woman? The best way is to try to be her friend first and then turn up the romantic overtones later. Showing your romantic interest in a woman right away upon meeting is one of the biggest seduction time-savers in this book. You *must* show your romantic interest in a woman right away, and she *must* know you are interested. There is no middle ground. Many men think that they have to establish a non-romantic relationship first before showing their romantic interest. They know that women want to feel safe, and understood, and truly loved as a human being before they take off their clothes and let a man degrade and despoil them. So lots of bonehead men take on becoming women's friends, figuring that then the woman will then know they are safe, that the man is a good guy, and will go nuts to have sex with them.

A bigger lie has never been told. The *worst* thing you can do in seducing a woman is becoming her friend first. At best it will slow down your seduction miserably, at worst (and most likely) it will *kill* your chances with her. It guarantees that she will eventually end up saying, "I wish I could meet someone just like you," but somehow not you. Here's why:

Women tell us that they decide about a man's status in their lives quickly—some have even told us that they decide in *the first minute* whether a man will be a hot lover or a lowly friend that they call for companionship when the real men are unavailable. Furthermore, if a man first establishes himself as a woman's friend, it'll appear odd to her when he "turns on the romance" later. She'll worry about "spoiling the friendship." She'll tell him he means too much to her to take that kind of a risk, and he will whine and only make it worse. If you've ever had this happen, it happened because you didn't show your romantic interest right away.

How to do it: You show your interest by doing the things a romantically interested guy would do. You establish eye contact with her and hold it a very small fraction of a second too long, you complement her in some way, perhaps by saying to the person who introduced you to her something like, "So this is the Jennifer you've been telling me about. She's even more beautiful than you said!" You also wink at her, feel free to smile at her, touch her casually (we'll discuss this later), talk about romantic things, and ask her about times she fell in love or felt romantic feelings. It is true that showing your romantic interest right away risks offending her, but here's the thing: remember, she's probably deciding about your status in her life right away. If you are acting like a romantic prospect, she'll have a natural tendency to put you into the romantic prospect category, because *thinking of you as a* *friend when you are talking and acting romantic would take an effort she doesn't want to make.* She'll fit you into the category you want because you are acting like you belong there. Act like a friend, on the other hand, and a friend you will become.

As another plus, when you show your romantic interest right away and she *does* get offended, you know not to pursue her! Imagine what it would be like to know in the first five minutes whether a woman was interested and you should pursue her, or not interested and you should dump her! This is exactly what you will have when you start showing your romantic interest right away by smiling, winking, touching casually, talking about romance and complimenting her.

3. MAKE REJECTION YOUR BEST FRIEND

I t takes balls to get laid, both literally and figuratively. Just like in business, you must foster the drive within yourself to succeed. You must keep your focus on the goal and not be sidetracked by the little details, like being rejected. The *only* way to have an abundant sex life is through rejection.

Many of our students feel crushed when a woman says "no." They get depressed and want to give up. Or they feel bad about themselves and think they are losers. We've also talked to guys who throw tantrums, get angry and blame the woman. These are natural reactions, but such reactions won't deliver the goods...sex. The bottom line is that when a woman rejects you,

you must take the long term view of things. Hearing "no" is part of the process of getting laid. When a woman says "no" you don't force her to have sex. This would damage your self-esteem, and could get you thrown in jail. What you do is go on to the next woman. You must train yourself as a dating commando to view and interpret all "no's" as steps along the way to your ultimate success.

Obviously it sucks to have a woman say "no." It also sucks to be spanking off in your room all alone. Remember: it isn't personal. Men ask, and women say "yes" or "no." Everyone, even seduction masters, hear "no" from women. They persist, and so must you. Even if it takes 1,000 no's for one yes, persistence is the only way.

If your goal really is to get laid, you must never, ever, ever give up. You may give up on a particular woman, but you don't give up on your ultimate goal of abundant sex. This never-give-up attitude is the key difference between a guy who is successful in seduction (or business, for that matter) and another guy who is at the whim of his emotions and fails frequently. The guy who doesn't let the rejection bother him succeeds, and the other guy fails. Which one do you want to be?

It is useful to view seduction as a numbers game. Keep in mind that even the most masterful seducers only pick up 10% of women they hit on. What they do is just keep on going and enjoy the process, like an adventure. You are learning a new art form, developing a new muscle, a new way of acting in the world and rejection will happen along the way. Be patient, for God's sake. No more whining.

Here are some things to remember:

• It isn't personal. Every man gets rejected some of the time.

• There are thousands of women who would be happy for you to fuck them tonight! You just don't know who they are and you give up too fast when you aren't willing to risk rejection.

• Today's "no" can eventually become a "yes"

later. Keep following the Rules in this book, and ask her out again some other day.

• Getting laid is a numbers game. A certain percent of women will say "no" and a certain percent will say "yes."

• Look at successful sports figures. Babe Ruth had the most home runs, but also had a huge number of strike-outs! Like Babe, you must be willing to swing for all you are worth and strike out sometimes.

• If you are rejected, just go on to the next woman. That's all there is to it.

4. Don't Share Everything About Yourself

Any man who tells a woman everything he is thinking and feeling is on his way to getting a Ph.D. in being an idiot. To tell a woman everything is suicide. Guess what? Women will often use men's most confidential and vulnerable information to hurt him later. They love to gossip, tease, or manipulate you for their benefit. Worst of all, a woman who knows all your problems will not sleep with you. You will probably scare her. Imagine that—you baring your soul so she won't think you are just a horny jerk, and you blow it anyway by sharing too much!

We learned the hard way about being idiots. Throughout both of our lives we tried to always be sincere, nice, open, honest, and emotionally available. Guess what? It didn't get us women. Do we have to repeat this a million times? Being Mr. Nice, Open and Honest will not get you nooky. This doesn't mean you should be mean, closed and dishonest. It just means you shouldn't share everything about yourself.

Here's the drill: Be fun and funny while still not telling her your darkest secrets. Share the parts of yourself she'll like and trust. When you first encounter any woman, her main concern will be finding out whether or not you are dangerous. You have to prove that you are safe. You don't want to come across as cold and remote by sharing nothing. You also don't want to come across as needy or overly sensitive by sharing too much about yourself. You have to share some, and convey a little cockiness and mystique so she will respect you and be intrigued.

Many men just try to go with the flow and not control conversations with a woman. However, that's when you get sloppy and start to talk about things you shouldn't. You start spouting off stupid opinions that turn her off and discussing controversial topics that drive her away. You must be aware of her reactions to topics you discuss and use this important information to push things to the next level.

Watch out. Topics like pornography and violence can often end up creating a conflict. Why risk offending her or upsetting her? You have only one goal here, getting sex, not making some huge political statement, or having her counsel you. Also, topics like murder, rape, etc., upset most women. Even if she isn't upset with you, she will be upset by the conversation and associate that upset with you. When she associates problems with you, it leads to more work and less sex. You must keep the mood fun, romantic, intimate, and easy, otherwise…you won't get sex.

Said another way: We have talked to men who think that women will desire them if they tell them about their childhood traumas, deepest pains, problems, and weaknesses. Save this type of discussion for your favorite group therapy session. It doesn't get you the girl. It only leads

to the women seeing you as a friend and thinking
you are a loser. It is up to you.

5. INITIATE, INITIATE, INITIATE

In these days of the wimpified man, many men come to us like scared and immature boys. They have forgotten that part of their job in life is to initiate flirting, sex, dates, romance, and everything else with women.

Another batch of "special" boys are upset that women don't offer their bodies up to them without pursuing and initiating. These guys think the world will serve them women on a golden platter and that they should be able to passively sit back and watch the women roll in. A rude awakening is about to happen if you believe this. Unless, of course, you a rock star or professional athlete. In this case, why are you reading this book?

You may also fall into the category of angry man.

This type of man vehemently resents women, especially the "horrible" facts of life that they must initiate dates, or suffer the fate of solo sex. They also complain that real feminist women should initiate sex half of the time. This type of bullshit, however, doesn't pan out in day-to-day life. The sorry facts are that it is your job to do all the initiating. Women probably won't call you back, and you have to be the persistent one. Women won't flirt with you on the street and you have to initiate conversations with them. Women won't offer their bodies to you unless you initiate and prove your worth to them.

You can resist and complain all you want, but it won't change anything. You must learn to get what you want and enjoy yourself in the process. If you want to be miserable, complain, be lonely, masturbate all the time and dream of dating porn stars from the confines of your home, do it. Stay alone, be a righteous son-of-a-bitch, and have a great time in the process. Be a resistant adolescent and see where it leads. The rest of us will be out flirting, taking chances, making fools of ourselves, and having hot sex. But yes, you have the right to be bitter.

Another option might be for you to purchase a blow-up doll, available for your physical needs 24 hours per day.

And then there is the option of initiating.

6. THE WOMAN CONTROLS THE SEX—ALWAYS

D id we mention that in some ways being a guy sucks? You can fight the fact that it's your job to pursue sex, and she has the final say, but you will always pay the price if you do. Getting sex is like looking for a job: you are the applicant and she is the employer. At any stage in the interviewing process, for any reason, she can dump you back into the ranks of the unemployed. You've got to get used to it.

To play the game of getting laid you've got to follow the rules, both the good and the bad, if you are to make them work for you. There's strong biological history behind a female having to know that a male has persistence before she'll mate with him. After all, she needs to know that he has the persistence to stay around and help take care of the children that he produces. Ever seen dogs mate? The bitch in heat waves her ass at the male, and he tries to mount her. She then snarls and snaps him off of her. He slinks back, then she displays for him again, and he tries to mount, and she snaps him off again. Biologists say that the bitch is selecting for a male who has enough persistence to stay around and who doesn't give up right away. Eventually she'll let him mount her—or she won't. It's the male's job to pursue the sex—the female has the final say.

Know this: a woman will often try to screw up a seduction like a female dog will bark off a male. One of our students was seducing a woman via email, and they were having lots of mutually satisfying sexual talk together. He suggested meeting in person, and she wrote back, "I must tell you, much as I am enjoying this, we will *never* meet in person." He took this in stride, kept up the erotic and romantic email with her, and several weeks later she suggested they meet in person. As he describes it, "In the first five seconds we were kissing, and then we went back to my house and had sex for hours." She had tried to screw it up, and by gently persisting he got to the "yes." Sometimes a seduction takes months of small persistent actions. Take them, and be on her schedule.

At the same time, it's incredibly important that you get it through your skull that she has the final say. You must cultivate an attitude that says, "if she doesn't want me, some other woman will, and I'm working on so many of them that I'm sure to score eventually." If one woman says a definitive "no," you thank her and move on. Keep following the rules and they'll start saying "yes."

When you are actually in bed with her or making any physical move on her, you must take her "no"s very seriously indeed. Remember that if a woman says you raped her, you will probably go to jail for a very long time whether you raped her or not. Go at her speed, and if she says "stop" then stop. Forcing a woman to have sex is the worst thing you can do. It'll put you in jail for a long, long time.

One of our students, for example, followed the rules with a woman he met and, after much work to create feelings of chemistry and sexual desire, he actually got her into bed. Unfortunately, she started to cry—never a good sign—and said she couldn't go through with it—she liked him, she said, but was a lesbian.

He was unhappy, frustrated, and horny. Then he remembered that she has the final say, and that it was the breaks of the game that sometimes it all fell apart. He talked with her a bit, did *not* pressure her, and she didn't come around. So he left, went home, and masturbated—ironically, he told us later, while watching a video of two lesbians having sex. Two weeks later he had his first success with another woman, then another, and hasn't looked back. "I'm so glad I didn't pressure her," he said. "A rape charge would have ruined my life."

If you are following the rules, you will never have

to force a woman to have sex with you, anyway. She'll want to. But remember the rules of the game: she has the right to change her mind, and the right to say "no." It doesn't matter how much work you've done to seduce her. Period.

7. Listen At Her

ichael took Debby to a jazz concert. All night long he talked incessantly about his job as a carpet salesman. He told her about the different types of carpet fibers, colors, corporate accounts, and information so esoteric even his coworkers would be bored. Whenever Debby discussed any subject she was interested in, Michael would go off on long-winded tangents, spouting off extreme opinions on every topic.

Michael is a typical Know it All, the type of Motor Mouth Man that drives women crazy. He fails to notice that the woman is left bored out of her skull, counting the moments until the date will finally be over. Even if this example is exaggerated, it's useful for you to look at your own life and interactions with women in terms of how well you listen.

Women have told us that the most important thing to them is for men to listen to their problems and stories, and to show a genuine curiosity about their opinions and lives, rather than simply focusing on themselves or on getting in women's pants.

When you stop talking and listen to a woman, you are demonstrating that you are a caring man, who values her for *her* (whatever that means), not just for her body. Listening is a service you provide women. In turn they will feel closer to you. In fact, they can talk and talk and talk, and you can get some good thinking time in. Just say, "Okay, yea, okay, wow" occasionally and she will likely be happy.

One caveat, when women are telling you about a problem at work, or a complaint about someone, or any other problem, don't try to solve the problem. Just listen. *Solving women's problems will cause you trouble,* and a fight will ensue. Let her have problems and just listen and stay out of the way.

If you are looking for a long-term relationship, it is especially important that you force yourself to listen on a daily basis.

Practice shutting up and listening when you are with women. It is fine to have an intimate conversation and share your opinions. It would be awkward for you to be silent in a conversation. On the other hand, it is crucial not to bore her with minute details of subjects she is uninterested in, and of your opinions on every topic under the sun. Be inclusive and *listen at her*!

8. PRACTICE WHERE YOUR EGO ISN'T ON THE LINE

Most guys make the mistake of putting their entire ego on the line when they interact with a woman they are attracted to. They try to start practicing seduction with the most beautiful, stripper-quality woman they can find, and are so tongue-tied that they can't do anything other than quiver and say stupid, humiliating things. Consequently, they end up feeling like totally worthless boneheaded idiots. The consequences of "messing up" are so big to their egos that they are tongue-tied and helpless.

You have to start you life as a seducer by practicing where the consequences aren't so great. Then, if you screw up, it won't matter so much. You won't feel like an idiot, and will be able to see the success that is inherent in *any* interaction with a woman. You'll be able to build on that success, and move up the ladder to more and more challenging women.

• **Start with women who aren't over-whelmingly beautiful.** The stakes are too high, from your ego's point of view, with a total babe or mega-fox. If you start with a woman a bit lower on the sexual-attractiveness scale, there will be less consequence to any screw up, and you'll be able to move on, and work your way up. It's good to practice with lots of women, anyway.

• **Practice with personals ads.** Personals ads are a great place to practice attracting women without feeling like you are too personally invested. Remember, in personals ads, you don't need to talk too much about yourself. Mostly, you want to describe some sort of romantic feeling, or scene, and then mention a little about yourself. For instance, don't write:

I'm lonely and need love! Sad divorced 33yo man seeks a woman who will be there for me! Brown hair and eyes, seeks woman 22-35. Bi OK.

You want to write an ad that makes her feel like *she'll* feel good, not like she'll be an appliance to meet your needs (she can find that out later!). The ad above is all about the guy, and meeting his needs. Take it from us, women who scan the personals don't care to hear about it. They want to know, what's in it for them? Consequently, write an ad that comes from **her** perspective:

Have you ever looked into someone's eye and felt totally connected? SWM 33, fit and attractive, willing to take emotional risks, seeks the right pair of eyes.

With personals ads, you can write letters back and forth, building slowly to talking on the phone, or meeting in person. This lowers the risk, and gives you a place to practice where your ego isn't on the line.

• **The internet.** The internet is the international

dating superhighway. And best of all, it's a great place to practice where there are no real-world effects on your ego. So what if a woman gets offended by your come ons on the net? Who cares? She just won't write you anymore. If you have an internet connection and are looking for low-risk practice spaces, this is it!

There is one important caveat about the women you will meet through personals ads or on the internet—they are very, *very* likely to be fat. Telltale signs are when they describe themselves as "rubinesque," or "very soft, curvy and feminine," "full-figured," or "well, I'm build like Delta Burke." While some men do meet thin women through these venues, it's best to think of them as practice arenas. But do use them, and do practice where your ego isn't on the line! Once you get used to being seductive, you can move up to the strippers and Victoria's Secret models.

9. NEVER EXPECT A WOMAN TO CALL YOU BACK

One of the most common mistakes men make is to think that a woman is not interested when she fails to return phone calls. As a result, guys will stop calling, whine about women's lack of responsiveness, and worst of all—give up. We know this is not intuitively obvious, but the fact of the matter is that women call when they feel like it. They don't act rationally. Remember, *a woman is not here to make your life easy or assist you.* Just pretend that women actually try to foul up your plans, and you'll be happier. You can complain about it, but as a dating commando, we now hold you to a higher standard. Your job is to keep going and not take it personally. You will be happier if you stop expecting women to make your life easier and call you back, ever.

10. ALWAYS BE PROSPECTING

A wise man once said, "There is no shortage of pussy; it's the delivery system that is the problem." You must improve the delivery system by constantly keeping your eyes, ears, and mind open to all women at all times. We assert that you are surrounded by available women all the time and you just don't realize it yet. To be successful with women you need to be clever, crafty, and aware of all options and opportunities.

"Always be prospecting" is one of the foundations of this book. Without the ability to be constantly prospecting, your chances of being successful are slim to none. Before taking our seminars and reading our books, many of our students stumbled through their days, prospecting no women, and having no sex. They constantly thought they were flawed in some way, never aware of the constant flow of sex available to every man as his birthright. If you read this book carefully and follow our advice you will be able to notice who the women are that you have contact with every day and turn many of them into lovers.

A man prospecting for sex is like a salesman prospecting for clients. Let's examine how a salesman tends to view life. To him, every situation poses the potential for a sale. A hungry salesman will do cold calls, ask his friends for leads, call up long lost relatives for leads, put ads in newspapers, and follow every lead to it's conclusion. In short, he will do whatever it takes to get the money. You too need this type of rigor and intensity on your quest for women.

Or you can think of your prospecting the way a deer hunter thinks about hunting. When a deer hunter sits in a tree stand for hours waiting for a deer to pass so he can shoot it, he constantly scans the landscape looking for any signs, smells, or sounds or sounds of his prey. He then aims his rifle, ready to go in for the kill. The hunter is patient and knows how to disguise himself so he doesn't scare off the animal, yet he is prepared at all times and has confidence in his skills as a marksman. You must now learn to be that hunter and that salesman, all at once.

Here is a list of places and situations that pose the potential for meeting women. The point is to open your eyes and notice the women you come into contact with daily. What follows is not an exhaustive list, but it will be enough to get you looking in the right direction.

Check out and talk to:

- Any woman who works in retail
- Female shoppers at grocery stores
- Women on the bus or subway
- Women in coffee shops
- Women in tattoo parlors
- Women in libraries
- Women at the gym
- Women in bookstores

- Women waiting in line with you
- Women friends know
- Women at concerts
- Women at museums
- Women in nature
- Women at dog shows
- Women at church
- Waitresses

Now, we must digress into an important tip. Many men fail to realize that there are lots of psycho women in this world. Psycho women are trouble for you. Psycho women are the ones who can be violent, a huge pain in the ass, time consuming, and who can even get you into legal trouble. Don't be naive and think that this type of thing could never happen to you. You must learn to avoid the psychos. One man we know was stalked by a woman he had dated, who went so far as to break into his home several times. It was very expensive for him to get rid of her. Another man dated a psycho for years. She loved to cry and every time he had sex with her, she would begin crying. Both of these men should have gotten rid of these psycho women early and saved themselves all the hassle.

To combat the potential damage psychos cause, you must learn to become a "psycho spotter." We train men to watch out for psychos while they are prospecting, and to keep away from them.

Stop prospecting a woman immediately if she:

• **Mentions being stalked or being a stalker.** A woman who has been stalked often attracts trouble. We are not trying to blame her or say she deserved it, but for some reason some women attract trouble, and you don't want to be near them. Also, she may well accuse you of being a stalker.

• **If your gut tells you to.** Most men don't trust their instincts. We say that your gut reaction is a valuable indicator to avoid trouble and keep you on track. Usually, your gut is a great guide.

• **If she cries while you are prospecting her.** Most women cry. This is not so bad in small doses. But a woman who cries constantly, or for no apparent reason, and early on in your interaction, is trouble. The trouble for you is that you will end up having to put out way to much energy and give her more attention than she is worth. Also, a woman who is crying will not sleep with you until she stops crying. This type of woman is not worth it.

- **If she mentions not liking sex.** A woman who mentions this is saying it for a reason. Typically she is saying that either she doesn't want you to only view her as a sexual object, which you must try to act like you aren't doing even though you are. Or she is saying that she truly doesn't like sex. If she doesn't like sex, get rid of her.

- **If she is an angry feminist.** If you think you can get away with sleeping with this type of woman once or twice, then do it, otherwise avoid them. They have a venomous streak in them for you just because you are a man. They will want to lecture you about women's suffering and the hardship of their lives. You can never win with a woman like this. If you do anything she will misconstrue what you did and fight with you. If you agree with her, you are admitting to being part of the problem because you are a guy. In the process you lose your self respect and her respect. She will then punish you for women's suffering. If you don't agree with her, she will fight with you, as well.

If you avoid the psychos, and talk to every women you can, you will have plenty of women to date, and eventually have sex with.

11. TIPS ON ASKING FOR HER PHONE NUMBER AND GETTING THE DATE

Once you are talking to a woman you are interested in you must ask her for her phone number. We've had students meet women, talk to them, charm them and then blow it by being too nervous to ask for her phone number. This is crucial.

Most women will rightfully not trust you. Once again, you must get into her head and world. For her, the world is a dangerous place, full of men who want to rape and hurt her. For her, even if she loves sex, it isn't worth it to risk her life with "another slime-ball man." To her you are just another asshole. Yes, you. You must prove your worth to her and prove you are not a psycho murderer.

Given that you need to get the phone number, and that she already doesn't trust you, you have to be crafty. You must first overcome her fear that you are a rapist. You do this by being patient, giving her your phone number, telling her where you work, and moving only a little quicker than her pace. You also may give her your business card; not because you think she'll actually call, but because having it helps her trust you.

If she says "no" don't fret and frown. Just keep talking to her and ask her again later. If you don't think she will say "yes" move on to the next chick. Remember, a "no" is not personal. The upshot of asking her for her number is that you are practicing, and every "no" gets you closer to your goal.

12. Don't Pin All Your Hopes On One Woman

As a dating commando you are creating a life of lush sexual abundance, in which you know at every moment that sex is readily available to you. This is not a pipe dream; it's actually a very do-able proposition. But on the way to having this life there are many traps you must avoid, traps that could inhibit your progress. Getting lazy and falling into the trap of pursuing only one woman at a time will eventually leave you with no sex at all—guaranteed.

The trouble starts when you become dependent on *one* woman for all your hot sex. And you will eventually become dependent on her. By only having one woman you don't leave any room for problems or mistakes, or variety. What if you get sick of her, then what? You are back to being alone. What if the sex stinks? Then you are alone. And what if you screw up? If you only have one woman in the hopper, then you will alone then, as well.

It is crucial to have many woman at once, all at different levels of seduction. One may be ugly and only available for a one night fling, another may be just at the beginning stages of flirting, another may be a stripper you just kissed for the first time. Without a variety of women in your life, you will get way too serious around your one and only hope, and will be so tense and nervous when you see her that you will probably drive her away. This is the same reason that people invest in mutual funds. They get the benefit of many stocks without having to worry about their whole lives falling apart if one of the stocks in the fund goes bad. Just as with stocks, with women you can't have all your energy tied up in one place. You need to spread your seed in many directions.

It is crucial for you to know that if one woman doesn't work out that there are others waiting in the wings for you. It gives you the confidence you need to truly score with women. The trap of serial monogamy is that you fall into committed relationships before you are ready. And it reinforces the idea that you must be committed to have sex. This is dead wrong. As a dating magnet you are playing with a wide variety of women always.

Don't let the simplicity of this rule fool you: pursuing more than one woman is an absolutely essential key to creating a life of abundant sex. The other rules will work ten times better if you follow this rule also. Conversely, the other rules will be ten times harder if you are stuck with only one woman, in yet another de facto relationship.

13. ALWAYS BE WILLING TO WALK

A man who is attracted to a women who proceeds to be a world class bitch has a choice to make. He can either "grin and bear it," hoping that if he's nice enough and sweet enough, she'll want to have sex with him. Or he can make it clear that her behavior is not acceptable, and demonstrate that he's willing to leave the relationship, to risk ever having sex with her, if she doesn't shape up. Which man do you think is more likely to get the sex life he wants?

If you are the man who "grins and bears it," you've probably been trained that a woman who will sleep with you, or give you any attention at all, is a rare, precious commodity. You've probably been trained that you have to put up with a lot of bullshit from her and treat her deferentially, approaching her as a supplicant. To some extent or another, you've learned that you have to be a woman's slave on the way to a sexual interaction. If you aren't, you'll offend her and lose her, and since there are so few women to choose from, you'd be a fool to screw it up by not putting up with her bull.

On the other hand, men who *are* willing to leave a relationship that doesn't work for them *are* able to get as many women as they desire. The truth is, women are a dime a dozen for a man who's willing to walk away from a relationship that isn't working for him. Most women will push a man to see how much shit he will take before he sets a boundary and tells her, in no uncertain terms, that it's *enough*. In this respect they are like men—everybody is always trying to figure out other people's boundaries, and to figure out how well they have treat other people. The man who isn't willing to walk tries to get laid by showing that he accepts her, no matter how big a bitch she is. The only result of this is that women don't respect him, avoid him, and it ends up looking like there aren't any women in the world.

Men who are willing to walk have power, and are willing to use it. This, in itself, is attractive to women. They want to be around a man who is in control of his life, and who isn't afraid of the consequences of having limits to what he'll put up with. Consequently, such men get *more* women than wimps do, because being willing to walk is *much* more attractive to them.

We knew a man who was the ultimate in being unwilling to leave a relationship. He was a university student, and was wildly attracted to a beautiful woman in his study group. Because she was so beautiful, she was used to having men at her beck and call, and was unimpressed by his submissiveness. When she needed something copied, he'd jump up and run to the copy machine for her, paying for her copies because she "forgot" her copy card. While he was getting the copies, she confided to the other people in the group that she was afraid he was stalking her, but when he returned with the copies, she thanked him and told him he was "so sweet." She ended up fucking another man in the group who didn't put up with her bullshit. The man who was her slave didn't get anywhere at all.

We are here to tell you that the truth is the opposite of what you learned. Women, we have found out, are "a dime a dozen," if you know what to do. Look: there are more women in the world than there are men. You are surrounded by them constantly. If you are willing to leave a relationship that isn't working for you—if you aren't so needy and insecure that you become a woman's slave—you can have your pick of them.

14. GET ONE NUT OFF FIRST

We've all been in situations where we've been so preoccupied with sex that we can't even think straight. We are sure you know what is like to stare at your date's tits for so long that you get absorbed in a fantasy and go into a daze. You get lost in a porn-movie fantasy with you and her in the starring roles. You date jostles you back to reality from your hormone-dazed fantasies, and you try to recover your cool. After cleaning the drool off your lips and unsuccessfully trying to think of something witty to say, you realize that being so preoccupied with sex caused you to blow it once again.

Being so horny that you can't think straight gives women the impression that you are a sex-crazed nut case, and makes her repelled by your presence. Your obvious sexual neediness turns her off as well, because you come across as a loser who can't get laid. Your neediness makes her wonder why she is with a loser like you in the first place.

If you are worried that you will be sexually preoccupied on a date, you must masturbate before going out. If you don't, your hormones will probably make you blow it, and you'll end up going home to whack off anyway. Getting one nut off first will leave you with a clear mind, and you'll be able to concentrate on the seduction, and steer conversations and actions towards sex. This is simple, but very few men take advantage of this age-old tip.

15. NEVER GROVEL FOR SEX

You know what? Some things are more important than sex. And, to a Man's Man (which is what you will become if you follow the Rules in this book), self-respect is far, far more important than getting laid. On the one hand, the more self-respect you have, the easier it is to get pussy. On the other hand, sometimes you can get sex by throwing away your self-respect, and groveling and begging a woman for sex. Our advice: don't do it. Ever.

Let's look at the typical groveling situation. Guy goes out with girl. Guy knows nothing or very little about seduction. Girl has nothing better to do, and allows some kissing and petting to happen. Girl gets turned off at some point, and decides she doesn't want sex after all. Guy begs with, "Aw, come on," "Why not," and "You don't know how it hurts a guy," until she finally gives in and let's him get on top of her for six minutes of unsatisfying—for her—sex. Afterward, she looks disgusted and tells him to get the hell out of her bedroom. She thinks he's a jerk and she wants to be thanked for doing him such a big favor. We feel ill just writing about it.

Groveling for sex may get you the girl—for a few minutes, at least—but it's not worth the cost. When you beg, cajole and pressure a woman for sex, you are most emphatically *not* being the kind of man you are most committed to being. Look at it this way: taking a long-term view of your relationships with women is much more useful than only thinking short-term. In the short term, groveling and begging might get you what you want, but the woman will hate your guts for it, and probably rarely—if ever—put out again. Meanwhile, by groveling, you have said something about who you are as a man. You have said that you are a groveler. And this will cost you.

What kind of a life does a groveling man have? Does he live life with a sense of abundance, joy, and freedom? Or does he live a life of fear of lack, restriction, and helplessness? We think you know the answer. When you grovel to a woman, especially around something as important as sex, you are taking on an identity of a fearful, helpless loser. *This hurts you.* The whole point of this book, in case you haven't noticed, has been to get you to think of yourself with self-respect. It's purpose has been to remind you, in case you didn't remember, that a man who respects himself is more attractive to women than one who is willing to betray himself to get a woman in bed. The groveler is the ultimate self-betrayer. He affirms himself as a loser through his behavior, and that sticks with him.

Meanwhile, the man who refuses to grovel, even when it might work to get him sex, affirms himself as a powerful man who can make real choices about his life. He may be masturbating tonight, but he knows that his standards and self-respect will make him the man he is committed to being, and ultimately give him the sex life he desires.

16. Be Sexually Imaginative

A man who's a dating commando has no sexual shame. This means you aren't ashamed of the fact that you like sex, and that you aren't ashamed of any of those fantasies you have, no matter what they are. As long as you are ashamed sexually, you'll be repressed. If you are repressed sexually, you will have a hard time getting a woman into bed. Also, you won't be much of a lover once you get her there.

So here's the bottom line: Almost everybody has sexual fantasies they are ashamed of. *Stop worrying about it!* Oh, we know, your fantasy is especially filthy. Believe us, we've heard it all. Your sexual fantasies that disturb you are not going away, so you might want to learn to live with them. Hell, you might even learn to have fun with them.

Not to complicate matters too much, but some sex therapists believe that our sexual fantasies are where the parts of us that we usually hide get to come out and play. For instance, a guy who doesn't want to dominate women may have sexual fantasies about dominating them, or a woman who is a committed feminist may have fantasies about being dominated. The things to get are 1) all sorts of fantasies are normal, and 2) just because you want to do something in fantasy doesn't mean you'll do it in real life on someone who doesn't want it. You're not bad; you're just a normal horny guy. Get over it.

Women have lots of repressed sexual fantasies, too, and are taught to repress them even more then men are. You can be the lover of her dreams if you are at ease with your own fantasies and can act out any of hers that she might desire. It's like playing dress-up as kids....if you are able to do it, a woman will sense it, and be more sexually open with you.

One important caveat: we are *not*, however, telling you to share your darkest sexual fantasies with her. She'll likely get scared of you, even once she's in bed with you, if you tell her fantasies outside of the "long slow waves-crashing-against-the-beach" variety. So, if you crave anything out of the norm deny it, at least at first. Just be open to any fantasy she may have, and be willing to play during sex with her. She'll give you more of what you most want and it will be much more fun for both of you.

17. Don't Be Her Therapist, Confidant, Or Buddy

The quickest way to fail with a woman is to be her therapist, confidant, or buddy. If you default in to these type of relationships with women, it is your funeral.

Being her buddy. Most men would have no problem having sex with a female friend and keeping the friendship intact. Men can usually distinguish sex as sex and keep it separate from relationships. Women, on the other hand, put men in two categories: lovers and friends. As a result, if you are too buddy-buddy with a woman she will automatically disqualify you as her lover. As we've said, you must make your romantic interest known right away and treat her as a lover from the get-go.

A man will also fail to seduce a woman if he doesn't "treat a lady like a lady." Men know this intuitively but tend to forget it when they are with a woman. A man doesn't treat a lady like a lady when he expects a woman to find his burps funny, or to appreciate his favorite fishing cap. When a man expects a woman to like and appreciate the same things his male friends appreciate, he is on the path of failure.

In the practical sense, treating a lady like a lady means:

• Dressing nicely when you see her.

• Being well-groomed.

• Not swearing as often as you would with your buddies.

• Opening the door for her.

• Behaving as a gentleman/treating her as if she is special.

Being her therapist. Some men try to seduce a woman by being her therapist. The man thinks that by giving her his advice on her problems and being Mr. Helpful, that she will reward him with sex. However, the opposite is usually true. What usually happens is that the woman associates him with the pain of her problems, and see him as a friend. She may even start to come to him for advice about other men she *is* having sex with. The guy is then stuck listening to her great sex life and remains like a horny dog, alone.

Being her confidant. Being a woman's confidant causes the same trouble as being her therapist. When a woman views a man as a friend, she disqualifies him as a romantic partner. Being a woman's confidant is worse than being her therapist because then she will say stuff like, "I'd love to have sex, but because we are so close already and I'd hate to do anything to lose your friendship."

The proper way to handle it when a woman tells you her problems is to appear to be listening attentively and nodding occasionally while you get some good thinking done about any other topic you chose. You should listen for a few minutes and then change the topic of discussion. It is okay to do this on occasion, but not too often. The key is to listen to her and not try to fix her problems. That is where the trouble starts. There's more on this when we discuss the rule "never fight with a woman," later in this book.

The reverse is also true. *A woman is not your mother, friend, or therapist* and you can't treat her or depend on her to fulfill those roles. Trying to get sex by having close women "friends" is a trap that wimp men fall into. If you look for a woman to be your buddy, therapist or confidant, the result will be that no woman will have sex with you. They will think you are a cute boy, but will never view you as a sexually passionate partner. Men will think you are wimp and not respect you. And you will know that you are degrading yourself respect by trying to get women by being a "nice boy." This tactic is used by men who haven't yet grown up. They still want their mommies, and expect women to take care of them.

If you tend to go to women for counseling and

women are your only friends, you must cut it out today. It may be painful at first, but must be done. One condition of being a man's man is that he has the respect of other men and is not dependent on women for sex or affirmation. Besides, it is your job to provide for women, not vice-versa.

If you tend to go to women for advice, counseling, etc., the best solution is to spend more time with your male friends. If you don't have male friends, get some. Men will give you advice from a male perspective on how to handle relationship problems and it will be a lot more straightforward and useful than most of women's advice. Realize that women are great, but only men know what is like to be a man. Men will joke with you, and bring out the competitive, outrageous, powerful, kamikaze spirit that you need if you are going to get laid. Be men's confidants, men's buddies. With women be powerful, passionate, exiting, romantic, intriguing and mysterious, and you will inevitably be their lovers.

18. MANAGE YOUR HYGIENE

Have you ever smelled something that was so disgusting that it made your stomach turn and thought you might puke? Maybe you stumbled upon moldy food, lots of dog shit, or a bathroom full of vomit. Well, this is what *you* are like to a woman when you don't bathe. It's true. Most women will never have sex with you if you do not manage your hygiene up to their standards. How you smell may not matter to you, but if you want to bag a woman, it is crucial.

Studies show that women are more sensitive to smell than men are. This means that you must be overly cautious and overly prepared if you want to get a woman. Just because you like how your pits smell after working out in the gym or after fixing your car, doesn't mean a woman will. Our research shows that 66 percent of women have been on dates where they would have had sex with the man if only he hadn't smelled bad to her. So, just because you are reading this thinking this rule only applies to other men, it doesn't. You, too, stink more than you should.

Also, you must do whatever it takes to never burp or fart in front of a woman who you are trying to seduce. Nothing, we mean nothing, turns a woman off faster than the smell of feces. Take care of your hygiene, and you'll be miles ahead.

19. USE CONDOMS

Condoms are "the law of the jungle." The world of a dating commando is dangerous enough without screwing around with extra risks. Remember, you can get HIV from one sexual experience. It can happen to you. Women do lie about who they've slept with and some infected women don't even know they have it. Let's put it this way: a woman who will sleep with you as fast as you'd like is the type of woman you should protect yourself from. 'Nuff said.

The other obvious risk is pregnancy. You do not want to get a woman pregnant. No woman, no matter how hot she is, is worth getting pregnant. You will be miserable if you get some one-night-stand slut pregnant, and if she keeps the baby it will cost you for the rest of your life. This means that you wear a condom. You do not trust a woman when she says she is on the pill. You do not "pull out" before you come. You do not trust her to keep track of her cycle, you do not trust her when she says she has no diseases, and you do not rely on her to take care of anything.

Sexually Transmitted Diseases (STDs) continue to be on the rise. A recent study of college students showed that 25 percent of all students had a venereal disease at the time of the study. STDs are not fun. Here's what will happen if you don't wear a condom: Just imagine that you have warts all over you cock. You try to urinate and you look down at big rid splotches and bumps the size of erasers. Whenever you pee it hurts, and your balls have swollen up like grapefruits. Or you meet a woman you really like and you give *her* a disease, and she hates you forever. Or you get herpes and you get those red sores on your cock for the rest of your life. Wear a condom and none of this will happen. Wear a condom.

Some men complain about condoms. We've heard men say that sex isn't as enjoyable with a condom and that it feels so much better without one. Some even say they won't have sex if they have to wear one. The truth is that no one likes to put on a condom. It feels a lot better to fuck without one.

However, this is not about what you desire in the short term. A Rules Man is committed to having a long life that he loves. If you do not use a condom and you sleep with a lot of women, eventually you will get an STD, a woman pregnant, or AIDS. You don't have to like using condoms, but you do have to use them. Get over your baby complaining. We are unwilling to sell you out and listen to you bullshit.

If you hate condoms one solution is to not have intercourse, and to stick to safer sex alternatives— oral sex and jacking each other off. While not 100% safe, you can use these methods if you won't use a condom.

20. WATCH YOUR BACK

Would you sign a contract a stranger gave you without reading it? Would you agree to give a hefty percentage of your income to a stranger for the next eighteen years? Would you participate in a crime that had a huge sentence with someone you didn't trust and hardly knew? Would you trust a stranger who told you that you had no chance of infection in the tuberculosis ward, and that you should ignore all the signs telling you to wear gloves and a mask?

Of course not, you are saying. What do we think you are, a fool? Well, we've got some bad news for you: you probably are, and have been, and will be again. This isn't you personally, though—it's all men, from time to time.

Men are naive to the point of imbecility when it

88

comes to the possible consequences of sex. While a man would never sign a contract a stranger handed him without knowing what's in it, that is exactly what a man does every time he has sex with a women without contraception. Stupid? You bet. Ever done it? A man would never sign over a percentage of his income for eighteen years, but in effect that's what he's gambling on doing when he has sex without birth control, as well.

How about committing a hugely illegal crime with a person you don't trust and hardly know? You risk this when you have consensual sex with a woman who flips out later and says you raped her. Dumb to not check out the person more thoroughly first? No question about it. Ever done it? Probably.

And walking into the tuberculosis ward without a mask and gloves because someone told you it'd be okay? Pretty dumb, but if you've ever had sex without a condom with a woman who you didn't know well and who hadn't earned your trust, you've done this, too.

The point is simply this: watch your back. Be as smart in sex as you would in the other situations listed above. Of course you can't isolate yourself from every risk, but don't think that she would never get pregnant and keep the baby, sue for child support, give you a sexually transmitted disease or accuse you of date rape. But what can you do without getting overly paranoid?

- **Follow your gut**. As we've said before, it's important to use your intuition to keep out of trouble.

- **Always use a condom**, no matter what she says about it not being necessary.

- **Become a psycho-spotter.** As we've said before, trouble seems to follow some women, and you want to get away from them before you become a part of it. If she complains about being stalked, is in and out of mental institutions, or has a history of taking legal action, keep away from her.

- **Get to know her.** If you really don't want to have to worry, get to know her well enough to make an informed decision about her character. It may take more time than you'd like, but actually liking the woman you are going to bed with makes it all more fun, anyway.

21. Cut Your Losses/Break Up Quickly

L ong, drawn-out dramatic breakups are the worst. They waste time and energy and end up pulling you off your path to abundant sex with lots of women. As a dating commando you are developing skills in being decisive, confident, and always going towards what you want. When there is trouble and you decide to cut a woman out of your life, do so without looking back.

In gambling you cut your losses to avoid losing more money. For example, you might lose $2,000 at a casino. When the dealer offers you the option of going double or nothing, the smart man cuts his losses and walks away. The same is true in business. If a businessman started a company and consistently lost money, he would be a flaming idiot for not getting out of that business and moving on to something that was better for him. Most of us are too stupid to take this same approach with a woman. We actually think things will change or improve if we stay in situations that don't work.

It is not usually "natural" for a man to break up quickly with a woman. Breaking up quickly usually seems cruel and nasty, but the bottom line is that it will cause her a lot less pain in the end if you lay your cards on the table and get rid of her quickly. She will be clear about your position and, even if she cries and makes a big scene, it will be easier for you both in the end.

When to do it:

• If she has constant emotional problems.
• If she wants to come between you and your buddies.
• If she interferes with your work.
• If being with her in any way degrades your self-respect.

- If she wants increasing amounts of time.
- If she steals money from you.
- If she likes to come over unexpectedly in the middle of the night.
- If she bites your cock.
- If she ever hits you.
- If you don't want to be her boyfriend and she wants you to be hers.
- If she stops giving you sex.

How to do it:

- Do it quickly.
- Don't comfort her. In her mind, you are the problem, so you *can't* be of comfort.
- Don't have sex with her for at least five months, or she'll try to restart the relationship.
- Don't be mean or cruel; it's not necessary, and better to be merciful.
- Don't hang around after you've told her. Get away from her at once.

It is easier on the phone. But if you've been sleeping with her for over two months, do it over coffee. If you break up in a public place she'll be less likely to throw a fit.

22. CONTROL ALL VARIABLES

Before you have sex with a woman, she has you on probation. In a way she's like a parole officer, looking for you to screw up or offend her in some way, so she can write you off and send you back with all the other horny guys. Why? It isn't because she's evil, or anything like that. It's because she, like everybody else, resists change. She will even try to stop changes that she would like.

People resist change. Her, you, everybody. Get into her world for a minute: her life is busy. She barely feels like she's keeping things together the ways things are now, and you want to *add* complexity to her life by becoming her lover? Forget it! She'll have a natural tendency to look at the downside more thoroughly than the upside...instead of imagining nights of hot sex, like you are, she's imagining you smelling, or farting, or trying to control her like her last boyfriend, or hitting her, or leaving your clothes around, or any of a myriad of problems that you could cause her.

So during those pre-sex meetings, she's waiting for you to do something that will disqualify you, so she can go back to her more orderly, controlled life.

This is precisely why you must control all the variables during a seduction. You must keep your goals in mind at every moment, and not waste time doing things that could accidentally alienate her. For instance, before having sex, a man may stupidly take a woman to a controversial lecture or movie, on a long drive where they may fight in the car, or to some other activity not directly related to seducing her. The problem with this is that spending too much time with a woman before you've had sex with her creates situations where something random may come up that convinces her that you are a jerk. After all, if you are seducing a woman, your job is to have that outcome in mind. Your job is not to entertain her, but to create romantic feelings in her, quickly, before she inevitably finds reasons to reject you.

It's amazing how easy it is to drift from this principle. One of our students had a first date with a woman, after which he kissed her. Instead of pursuing a romantic agenda with her, and taking her somewhere special to create more romantic feelings, he took her rollerblading on their next date. The moment she saw how badly he rollerbladed, she lost all desire for him, telling him that she only liked men who were more athletic. He didn't keep control of all the variables, and he lost the sex he was building. If he would have taken her someplace where he could demonstrate his skill in something else the date would have turned out much better.

Think of yourself as a salesman: you are not in front of your client to hang out and party; you are there to create situations in which he buys your product. Dating is the same way, and by allowing your focus to drift, you don't control all variables and can lose the hot tamale you are coming closer to bag and bed.

24) Tips On Asking For The Date

So you've got a woman in mind. How do you ask her out? Most men fail at this point because they don't know how to ask a woman out in a way that gets a "yes." By following these tips and techniques, you'll have the confidence to ask out any woman you want.

• **Be brief on the phone.** When you call her to ask her out, keep the call short, especially if you think you might mess things up. It's far better that she have just enough data about you to fantasize about how wonderful you might be, rather than to have too much data and discover something that puts her off.

Be friendly and smile while talking to her (smiling changes the quality of your voice, and helps even on a phone call).

• **Always have a specific idea in mind for the date.** As a dating commando, you *never* ask a woman out, either by phone or in person, without having a specific idea of what you might do and where you might go. "Specific" means that you have a precise location in mind. "Dinner" is not specific. "Dinner at Italiano's" is specific. You don't say, "So, uh, wanna go out to dinner sometime?" You do say, "Hey, I heard about a wonderful little place called "Italiano's" that people say has a great feel to it. I wonder if you'd like to go there with me sometime?" You don't say, "wanna see a movie sometime?" You do say, "I noticed the film *Don Juan De Marco* is playing downtown. I'd love to go there with you sometime." Have options available, and never make her supply the details.

• **Don't be too available.** When she says "yes," then you have to set up a time. It's important to not be too available...the worst thing you can say is, "Oh, anytime," because she will think you must be a loser with nothing to do and wonder why she would be going out with you. You must appear busy, so that she understands that you have a lot going on in your life (even if you don't), and that she's lucky to be a part of it. Also, don't rely on her to think up times to get together. Instead of saying, "So when's good for you?" take charge. Say, "Tuesday evening at seven will work, or perhaps Thursday, but a little later."

• **Make decisions.** You don't want to be a control freak, but you don't want to be a useless wad of indecisiveness, either. You never say, "Oh I don't know, what do you want to do?" You make decisions. This means that when those little meaningless choices come up during the date— such as what table to sit at—you decide quickly and easily. If she'd rather sit somewhere else then you can say "sure," but always make decisions quickly when you are with her. This shows her that you are guy who is in charge of his life and not wishy-washy, and will put you miles ahead of most of the other guys she meets. This seems obvious or simple, but it sets the stage for seduction.

- **If she says no.** As we've said before, some rejection is inevitable, and your ability to endure it is your key to sexual prosperity. If she says "no", all it means is no. It does not mean that you are a bad guy, or worthless, or stupid, or any of the other things that guys like to tell themselves. We suggest that you create an interpretation that empowers you, such as "perhaps she has a boyfriend," or "maybe she just wasn't feeling well," or "I guess she's really caught up in her own world," or even "Perhaps I'm not her type." Also, look at what you learned from the interaction, and try again on the next woman you meet. A rules man is able to view every situation into a learning experience and a success.

When you are talking to her, you have to talk romantic. Here are a few of the best seduction questions; when you ask them, they make her think about romance, re-experience romantic feelings. In time, she'll connect those feelings to you. These questions are most useful when you pepper them in throughout a conversation. If you stack many together it will often sound stupid and she'll know you are trying to get into her pants. When you use them sparingly they greatly aid in your seduction.

The top four seductive questions are:

1. Have you ever _____?

Fill in the blank with descriptions of emotions you want her to feel with you, like "fallen in love," "felt very romantic," "really felt like letting go and doing something crazy," "experienced love at first sight," etc.

2. What is it like when_____?

Fill in the blank with the same kind of thing: "fallen in love," "had a great date," or "felt full of desire, etc.

3. Can you recall a time when_____?

Fill in the blank with your favorite romantic phrase.

4. What was your best_____?

Fill in the blank with thinks like "kiss," "sexual experience" (if you think she won't get offended), "romantic date," "wildest vacation," etc.

Women in large cities will rarely give you their number. Why should they? You must "accidentally" show up repeatedly where they work or hang out to establish your credibility, or give them your number, or set up a date right then.

When you finally do get the date, know ahead of time that she probably won't show up. This is fine; women not showing up is all in a day's work for a dating commando. You still have a 20 percent chance that she will show up, though, so don't despair. We recommend setting up the date in the neighborhood where you meet her initially; it helps her feel more comfortable with you if she sees you in a similar environment to where you first met. Also, make the date for sooner rather than later; the further in the future the date is, the more unlikely it is that she will show. Coffee dates are the best first dates. They give you a chance to find out more about her and gets her used to the idea of being romantic with you, before you go out with her at night.

A less intrusive approach is to get her email address. This is almost better because you can slowly seduce her in cyberspace while still retaining an image of being non-intrusive and safe. You can send her romantic poetry and seduction letters until she is practically begging for you.

The following are examples of possible things to say when asking for the date. Say these things after you have been talking to the woman for at least a few minutes, and have already have developed a connection with her and she already shows some signs of being interested. Just going up to a woman and asking her out cold will rarely work. When you ask her out, use the information you already know about her to customize you approach. If you meet her in a bookstore, for example, ask her to a book reading or to a bookstore cafe. If you meet her in a bar ask her to a band or another bar, etc.

So here are some lines:

• "It has been great fun talking to you. It is rare that I meet a woman so intelligent and clever. I have to leave now, but I'd love to talk again. Can I call you some time? What is your phone number?"

• "I can tell that you are into having exciting and intensely romantic times. I hear [band] will be in town next week and I have an extra ticket, would you like to come along with me and some friends? I can call you later to set up the details. What is your number?"

• "I never do this, but you just seem so wonderful that I am risking looking like an idiot to ask you out. Would you like to go out some time?"

"I am really surprised at how easy it is to talk to you and be with you. I'd hate to not have that again. When can I see you again? What is your phone number?"

What not to say:

"Uh, ummm. I'm not sure how to say this.

Umm. I think your tits are really big and you look like you'd be fun to fuck. Can I call you for phone sex?"

With practice you'll be asking women out and having more dates than you can handle.

24. Kissing Her For The First Time

Ah, the first kiss. Not so hard once you know what you are doing, but a seemingly insurmountable task if you don't.

If you are following the rules, the first kiss will be easy because she will be thinking about it, too. Don't think that women don't want it. And don't think that she doesn't know that all you want is to kiss her and get her in bed as soon as you can. She knows. You are not pulling one over on her.

A guy runs into problems when he doesn't show his romantic interest right away, so the woman he asks out thinks of him as a friend. He's also wishy-washy and unprepared when he asks her out, says "oh, I'm free anytime," then ends up taking her to the same kind of place he'd go to with guy friends. He generates zero romantic feeling, ignores the little things, doesn't make her feel special in any way, and then wonders why it's so hard to go in for the first kiss. We'll tell you why it's so hard for him: because he's done everything wrong, and has about a 1% chance of success.

Let's contrast this with a guy who's followed the Rules. He's showed his romantic interest right away to every attractive women he's met. Some have been unresponsive, some have been mildly responsive, and some have been very responsive. He's asked out the most responsive ones, having specific date ideas in mind when he asked. He wasn't too available, was decisive, and kept his outcome in mind.

He takes his date somewhere romantic, like local public flower gardens, complements her beauty, talks about romantic things, holds open doors for her, and treats her like a lady. His car is clean, he looks nice, and smells good. He's frequently touches her casually, and looks into her eyes, and winked at her a few times. He's created a world just for the two of them, and when he goes to kiss her, she's ready and open. It may "seem to just happen," or she may even kiss him!

Having said all that, here are some pointer for getting that first kiss:

• **Have established a precedent of touching her.** If you've followed the other rules and have touched her casually during the date, you'll have learned how interested she is. If she recoils from your touch, then you probably need to create more romantic situations for her first. If she doesn't respond or responds positively, then she's showing signs of accepting your touch and is more likely to respond positively to the kiss.

• **Have looked into her eyes.** As we've said before, looking into her eyes and holding the gaze a fraction of a second too long is an important step in seducing a woman. If she always looks away, or looks angry, she probably doesn't want you to kiss her yet. If she seems okay with it, then you can probably proceed on to the kiss.

• **Do the "fake out."** Sometimes it helps to ready a woman for your first kiss if you earlier move towards her, slowly, like you are about to kiss her, then "change your mind" and move away. Remember, if you are following the Rules she probably wants you to kiss her anyway, and doing the "fake out" primes her even more. Faking her out shows her that you are in charge.

• **Say the right thing.** What you say when going for the first kiss is up to you, but here are some options. Some men chose to not say anything, which can work, though we must tell you that to kiss a woman without her permission can be construed as sexual assault.

While from a legal perspective you are better off asking a woman before you kiss her (with something like "may I kiss you?"), a number of women have told us that they find men who ask before the first kiss to be a complete turn-off.

Some have even said it makes them angry when a man asks first. Welcome to the world of being a man, where to not ask can get you arrested and to ask can get you rejected. Our students have had good luck with saying something like, "Don't panic, I'm about to kiss you" while moving in for the first kiss. Such an announcement gives her an opportunity to stop you if she wants, but tells her rather than asks her about the kiss.

• **Be physically prepared.** Make sure your lips are soft and your breath is good. Also make sure you don't have five-o'clock shadow. Use conditioner when you shampoo your beard, if you have one.

As you master the tips in this rule, you will find that you get to chose when the first kiss occurs...and more!

25. For Long-Term Relationships: Sacrifice

If you are going to have a successful long-term relationship with a woman, you must know ahead of time that you will have to sacrifice to make the relationship work. By design, relationships with women are work. If all you want is just to get laid and have fun all the time, don't be in a relationship. Relationships are nurturing for men and can provide deep joy and satisfaction, but they are not a cake-walk.

Sometimes our students have commented on feeling resentful towards their girlfriends. These men have not accepted that they will have to make sacrifices to keep the relationship working. They go into relationships naively pretending that they will not have to change themselves or their behaviors.

Your life will be easier if you accept ahead of time the sacrifices that you will be expected and forced to make. Expect to sacrifice: time, money, energy, personal desires, peace and quiet, watching every football game, total freedom, other women, and the right to complain.

Remember, relationships are a job and must be treated as such. Your boss often expects you to sacrifice: you may not want to come into work at 7:00 am, but you must do it for the job. What about all the overtime you work, or the way you kiss your boss's ass for a raise, or the way you reorganized your vacation time because the job needed you? A relationship is just as demanding, if not more so.

We are not saying that you need to be pussy-whipped and do everything you wife tells you to do. We are not telling you to give up your self respect or do things you fundamentally disagree with. What we are saying is that you must keep your girlfriend happy to an extent, and provide for her in a way that works for both of you. When you become her boyfriend or husband you give up the right to get everything you want and take on the responsibility to provide for your wife support, energy, money, love, and so on.

26. For Long-Term Relationships: Always And Forever Find New Ways To Delight Her

I t's as if men have a checklist. They get a job, and stop thinking about it. They give a home, and stop thinking about it. They get a stereo, and stop thinking about it. They get a girlfriend, and stop thinking about it. Big mistake, if you want to keep her.

It seems like men get lazy after they get a woman to fall in love with them. They forget that they have to keep her falling in love with them over and over, or the relationship will fall apart.

If you are in a relationship, you must learn to keep your woman happy by continuously providing her with new opportunities to fall in love with you all over again. This means always and forever finding new ways to delight her. Keep thinking of her as a woman you are just starting to date, and behave accordingly. Set up "dates" with her as if you were new to each other again. Keep asking yourself, "What would really make her happy?," just as you did at the beginning of your relationship, and *do those things!* Don't slack off, or you will find yourself with a relationship that gives you no joy and a woman you don't like.

This is not such a tall order. There are plenty of couples that focus continually on making life wonderful for the other. You can do this, too. You simply have to keep at it.

Actually, having a girlfriend is not that much different than having a job, after all. If you don't keep providing new and better value for your employer, you won't advance in the company, and you'll be the one laid off at the next downsizing. *In anything in life, you are either adding value or taking value away.* You have to be a value-adder to have any kind of relationship grow.

You can keep romance alive by constantly doing the "little things," like giving her little gifts, cards, and saying things like "I love you." You can learn massage and massage her, or compliment the way she does her hair. You can also keep your less romantic parts away from her; don't fart or burp around her, or get too sloppy in the way you dress.

"But wait!," we hear you cry. "This makes a relationship into work!" Yes, it's true; but it also creates a relationship in which she feels lucky to have you and gives you all the sex you want. It's a good trade-off, we say.

27. Always Act With An Outcome in Mind

I t is important to have a goal for every interaction with a woman. The goal should be realistic, yet a stretch as well. This approach will help you achieve any result you want to produce.

Life for the sloppy seducer is a series of unplanned mishaps, emergencies, crises, and bad surprises. The master seducer, however, carefully plans for success and is not pulled off-course when inevitable mistakes happen. He enters every situation with women with a clear outcome in mind. While on a date, his goal may to make the first kiss or first sexual interaction. In a coffee shop, his outcome may to flirt with two women and get one phone number. Whatever the situation, the goal must be clear in your mind. If not, the woman will get mixed messages from you, and you will get sloppy.

Do you think football players show up to a game to simply "see what happens?" They obviously show up to kick ass, score points, and win the game. A salesman gives presentations and sales calls with the direct outcome of ultimately selling more products and make more money. In your life you don't show up to work just to putter around and do what feels good. You have an outcome, a task that must be accomplished no matter how slowly or ineffectively you accomplish it.

You must create your own scoreboard for your dating interactions. Most men take dating, flirting, and seduction way too casually. We recommend you keep yourself goal oriented in seduction and always have a clear and measurable outcome. Make these outcomes appropriate for each situation you are in. It may not be realistic for you to have sex with a woman after going out for coffee once. It may be better to focus on kissing her. The outcome is there to keep you on track and empower your ultimate sexual goals, not act as a baseball bat to hammer over your head every time you blow it with a woman by setting your sights too far from your level of mastery.

If you finally surrender and take our advice you will be 100 times more likely to achieve your goals. So take out a pen and write on your arm, "I always act with an outcome in mind, this will get me sex with hot babes." Then go out and score!

28. Avoid Fighting With A Woman

You can never win a fight with a woman. If you do, she'll cry, or flip out, and you will be the loser. While sometimes it seems that women were put on this planet to piss you off, fighting with women is not useful. It makes you seem like an unstable jerk and it won't get you laid. This rule says that you must pick you battles carefully and recognize that you pay a high cost when you fight.

One thing to keep in mind is that women love problems. Whether it is a job conflict, relationship problem, or other problem, they love the drama. Women love to talk about their problems and even bond with each other through them. Men don't. We like to solve problems. The problem is that women usually want to be heard by a man, not fixed. This is another entrance into conflict. If you solve a woman's problem, you become her problem.

Fighting with a woman is very different than fighting with your buddies. You need to be tactful with a woman, and not so with your friends. You can tell your buddies to "shut the fuck up," or "give me a break. Get out of my face or I'll knock you on your ass!" You say that, they stop, and you all get back to watching the game and drinking more beer. Problem solved.

Women aren't like this. With a woman, you must watch what comes out of your mouth very carefully. Many of the things you say in a rage will be used against you and will be things you regret and feel guilty about. It is in *your* best interest to watch it so you won't pay a hefty price later when she uses it to control you or make you feel like a heel. Worst of all, if you don't watch your mouth with a woman she will probably punish you by not putting out until you buy her something expensive, or apologize to the point where you sell yourself out.

If you are angry with a woman, you must first decide if it will improve your situation to tell her. For example, if you are angry that she had coffee with a former boyfriend, it is best to keep that information to yourself. It would be better to tell her that you also ran into a former girlfriend and you were considering going out with her. Ask what your girlfriend thinks of the idea. She will say you shouldn't do it, of course, and you've made your point.

It is also not useful to tell a woman about how upset you are that she ruined your favorite workshirt. To her it was a cruddy old shirt, and she couldn't care less. To complain to her will make no difference at all.

It may be useful to tell her about how it upsets you when she wakes you up early on Sunday mornings at 7:00 am, when it is your only day to sleep in. When you express your anger at her, it is crucial to use many specific examples and make requests of her to stop doing a specific behavior or behaviors. (If you just want to yell at her just to vent, it won't work. See the rule "blow off steam away from her" for guidelines on this.) Here are a few good phrases you can use:

"When you wake me up at 7:00 am, I feel upset because I feel like you don't respect my days off work. I enjoy sleeping in on Sunday's because it is my only day off. If I catch up on my sleep on Sunday's it makes it easier for me to give you everything you want. I request that you let me sleep until 8:30 am on Sundays from now on."

If you find yourself in constant conflict with a woman, something is wrong with the picture, and it is usually you. It means you are not properly sacrificing for the relationship, or she is a psycho who you should get rid of, or it means that you need to look at why you are such a hot head and quit it.

If you ever experience rage around a woman, you must get yourself out of the situation. It is *totally* unacceptable, at any time, to hurt her physically. Even yelling at her and insulting her is a sign that you should get away from her. You should also get away from any woman who attacks you physically. Even if you just have a strong intuition that she is going to hurt you, get away from her. It is always better to be safe than sorry.

30) HAVE STYLE

Think of a man who is attractive to women. Perhaps it's John Travolta, in the movie "Get Shorty." Perhaps it's a rock star you admire. Perhaps it's someone else that you see on the street. As you imagine him, put yourself in a woman's place for a moment and ask yourself, "what does his style say to women?" It probably says something like, "you want me," or, "I'm successful and attractive."

Now think of a man who is unattractive to women. Think of how he dresses and moves. Through his style and behavior, this man also conveys a message to women. A man whose dress is sloppy, gawdy or tacky sends a "go away, you don't want me" message to women. The message may even be hostile: some men dress and move in a way that is so unattractive to women, their message can only be understood as, "Fuck you, women!"

Now think of yourself, dressed as you usually dress. What message does your style of dressing convey? Does it say, "I prefer looking sloppy to actually getting laid"? Does it tell women to go away? Or is your style inviting and attractive to women?

If you want to get laid, you have to develop a style that says "you want me" to women. You may not have that style now. Here's how you do it:

• **Model men who's style you admire.** If you know someone who always looks good, ask him what he does, and how he would dress differently if he were you.

• **Look at men in the media who dress well**, and emulate them.

• **Go to clothing stores** and ask the people who work there to help you with a "new look." Be willing to try on and wear something that you normally might not buy.

• **Get a woman to help you**. If you know a woman who has a terrific sense of style, ask her to go shopping with you, and buy what she tells you to. Then get into the habit of wearing what you bought.

• **Learn to move well**. You don't have to be Fred Astaire, but you should get in the habit of walking tall, being light on your feet, and moving like a man of consequence and confidence. If you are in the habit of shuffling as you walk or slouching, or if your body is tight and rigid, you may need to invest in some bodywork like massage or Rolfing to open your body up to moving more easily. You may also want to start doing yoga or Tai Chi. These exercises will relax your body. Both the authors of this book have had lots of massage and other bodywork, and it has, without question, made us more attractive to women.

• **Emphasize the little things**. In every stage

of seducing a woman, details are everything. Have a nice belt, clean good shoes, and clothes that fit well and are clean and pressed if necessary. You know how much you like it when a woman has every little detail of her appearance as sexy as possible—now it's time for you to take care of the details of how you look and become sexier for her!

As you explore style, you will begin to discover which styles are "you" and which aren't. You will develop a "look" that will do a marvelous job expressing who you really are. Having such a style helps in every area of life, because people want to interact with a together, self-expressed person. You'll have better luck with women, and in other areas of your life as well.

30. NEVER HIT A WOMAN

We've said it before, but this rule is so important to your self-respect, long-term success with women, and staying out of jail that we've made it into a rule of its own. *Never hit a woman!* When you hit a women, on a moral level, she has won. You have lost it and are the perpetrator, and she's a victim. Hitting a woman is wrong, illegal, and contrary to being a Rules Man. See *Avoid fighting with a woman* and *Blow off steam away from women* for more tips and tools for handling conflict with women correctly.

Never hit a woman! Never hit a woman! Never hit a woman!

This is crucial!

31. Blow Off Steam Away From Her

Of course you'll get mad. Life is aggravating. Women are aggravating. *You* are aggravating. Sometimes it seems like we have a container inside of us, and the bullshit of life fills it and fills it until the container is full, and we can't take any more stress. In those times it's important to be able to "blow off some steam" and vent your feelings of frustration so you can be more relaxed and get on with your life.

"Blowing off steam" is a great thing to do, and people should probably do more of it, but innumerable problems are caused by men who blow off steam improperly. You will never become a Rules Man if you don't learn to manage your anger. Blowing off steam calms you down so you can focus on seduction and not be caught up in anger. Here are some guidelines for blowing off steam in ways that don't blow your life:

• "Blow off steam" where there are no real-world consequences. Okay, we understand that sometimes you need to punch something. So do we. The thing to do is to punch something where there are no bad consequences from the punch.

Men are famous for blowing off steam in ways that hurt people. For instance, punching a wall is wrong, because it breaks your hand and messes up the wall. The consequences are big and stupid. You should punch a punching bag, or a bunch of pillows, or something that won't hurt you back. Other men smash things. Well, that's fine, but if you are going to smash something (which can be very satisfying and downright therapeutic), smash something 1) that you own, 2) that you don't like, and 3) that is, preferably, broken already. And, of course, smash it in a way that doesn't hurt you. It's perfectly all right to get out your work gloves, safety glasses, and hammer and take out your pent-up rage on your old, broken VCR. Just do it in a way that doesn't hurt you, or property you care about. Hell, go out and smash bottles on any nearby railroad tracks. It is great to hear glass smashing against metal, rock, and wood.

• Don't blow off steam around people who won't understand what you are doing. If you blow off steam around people who don't know what you are doing, you'll appear dangerous, scary, or psycho. Blow off steam where no one will freak out—your basement can be a good spot.

• Don't blow off steam around the people who made you mad in the first place. Remember what we said above about blowing off steam where there are no real-world consequences? If you pound on something while yelling and the woman you are mad at can hear you, she'll be scared and angry and there will be lots of unpleasant real-world consequences for you.

• Have buddies with whom you can let your

opinions and judgments loose without restraint. Having guy friends you can kick back with and say anything you want is a great way to let off steam about people who are upsetting you.

• Blow off steam when doing physical activity. One of our students yells obscenities at people he's mad at while splitting logs with an ax. Another pretends he is stomping on the people who have frustrated him while he runs. By venting these feelings in imagination, they are more able to be relaxed and appropriate with these people in real life.

After you blow off steam safely, it'll be easier for you to contain yourself with women. A powerful man creates situations in which he can vent all of his anger safely, and not hurt anyone. Do this rather than venting at the woman you are dating.

32. MAKE IT LOOK LIKE YOU ARE NOT WORKING

What is the one difference between seducing a woman and having a job? While at work you need to look like you are working—in fact, the harder you look like you are working, the better it is.

When seducing a woman, the opposite is true: when you are with a woman, you absolutely must make everything look easy, even if you worked hard to set up the perfect romantic evening, or hunted for hours to find the perfect little romantic gift.

A common stupid mistake a man makes is to expect a woman to acknowledge and thank him for all the work he's done in seducing her. This is suicide for the seduction. A woman will rarely, if ever, acknowledge that you have pursued her, called her, created good feelings for her, risked rejection in asking her out, risked rejection in touching her for the first time, kissing her, and every other initiation that you've made. After all, the seduction seems to be happening effortlessly for her, isn't it? It must be effortless! You will be happier to not even expect a woman to understand what you have gone through to make the romance seem effortless. She won't appreciate it anyway. It is best to boast to your friends and show off for them later.

Bringing up the fact that you are putting in effort that she isn't appreciating will offend her. Look at it this way: she expects romance to happen, and the last thing she wants is a guy plotting how to get her. If you tell her about the work you are doing to seduce her, you break the magic spell and she will accuse you of treating her like an object, not really caring about her as a person, and be angrier than you can possibly imagine.

Make it look like you're not working, and the women you desire will be yours!

33. MAKE IT WORK FOR YOU

You must make every situation work for you, otherwise you will go through life miserable. If you want to be the king of the jungle you must bring out that cocky confident attitude in yourself. This attitude integrates planning for both the worst- and best-case scenarios. You must be asking yourself, "How do I enjoy myself no matter what happens?" The commando is always prepared and plans to have fun alone, with buddies, while getting laid, everywhere. The man who really masters this attitude is an unstoppable monster in life who has the balls the size of Texas, tons of sex, lots of fun, and accomplishes whatever he sets his mind to.

Making it work for you is about having an

attitude that is optimistic, yet realistic, in all situations. It is very simple: you look for how you can enjoy yourself to the maximum in each situation, and create the conditions for that to happen. For example, if a woman blows off a date with you at a coffee shop, you make the situation work for you by reading your favorite seduction book, flirting with the cashier, getting work done, etc. If you get upset and pout, then you didn't make the situation work for you, you were a victim (again).

One of our students had hours of painting to do on his new house. On the way home from the paint store he realized he had forgot to bring his boom box—he had planned on listening to baseball all afternoon while he painted. When he realized he forgot his radio he went to near by friend's house and borrowed one, rather than doing without. By taking the time to make the situation more bearable, he made it work for him.

Another component of this attitude is the ability to say how a situation will go, even before you know how you will accomplish what you have said. You set your intention, play full out, and get the result. This is useful to do in both business and dating situations: the commando sets his intention at the beginning of an evening. Perhaps he decides to talk to six women, flirt with twelve, get three numbers, and fuck one. He makes the situations he is in work by having a persistent unstoppable attitude. He is living on the edge in an exciting, intense manner.

Many men complain that dating is too hard. These same men complain that life is too hard, as well. They tend to become victims of circumstance and be at the whims of everyone else but themselves. For example, if a man believes that there is a scarcity of sex, he will act out of desperation, rather than making the situation work for him. If he has sex with a woman until 6:00 A.M. because he thinks this will be his only opportunity, even though he has a 7:30 A.M. presentation at his job the next morning, he messes up his life and has not made the situation work for him. He has made himself a victim of the situation.

The following are questions you can ask yourself to make any situation work for you.

• What do I want to have happen in this situation?

• What will I do that will be fun if I "fail"?

• How can I make this situation work for everyone?

• What would make this situation most fun?

• Why am I a god who deserves all good things?

• What will I do to "reward" myself for getting through this situation?

• What am I most committed to in this situation?

34. Don't Expect A Woman To Have Integrity The Same Way You Do

Realizing that women do not have integrity the same way you do will solve lots of problems when you are with them. By design, women don't see integrity the same way men do. We could pull out all sorts of psychological and sociological studies and bore the shit out of you, but the bottom line is that women approach integrity and have different definitions of it than men do. This is one area where men get pissed off at women all the time, and wreck their chances of getting laid.

For most men, we say we will do something or give our word and we either keep our word, or communicate that we won't be keeping our word. If we break our word we apologize and fess up to it. As you've probably noted as you've dated women who are late to dates, who don't show up, never call back, etc., women don't. Most women are driven by their feelings more than by their word. It's more important that everything feel right than to proceed if it doesn't. What this means for you is, when she doesn't show up for a date, she doesn't mean it the same way you would.

Even though it may be hard to accept, you *must* accept women as having a different type of integrity. One of our students had a pet peeve regarding women being late for dates. He would get upset and chew them out when they finally showed up. We told him to chill out and just accept women the way they are. You don't do this for her—you do it because it makes *your* life easier. You can stop stressing, looking at your watch every second, wondering if you showed up on the wrong date, etc. Just relax and hit on another woman until she shows.

Remember, women don't have integrity the same way you do.

35. Rules For Handling Women Younger Than You

What a surprise! You want to date women who are younger than you! But how is this accomplished?

It is possible. Here's what you need to know:

• **Some young women are more into older men than men their own age.** Remember, if you want to be dating 19 and 20 year olds, you competition among the men her age is, in many ways, pretty lame. These guys have the emotional sophistication of a watermelon, no car and zero dollars, a hormonally-mediated inability to cuddle, and are clumsy lovers at best. You, on the other hand, are pretty much like that, too, but the 19 and 20 year old girls you want to date don't know that yet. You can use this to your advantage.

What you're going to be looking for is the young women who believe that older men are different than the young ones, and who see your age as a benefit, not as a liability. Such young women do exist. There are also young women who see your age as a liability, and your interest in them as proof of some dark intent. You must learn to tell them apart—you'll rarely have success with the women who are suspicious of you, but the ones who are naturally curious and interested in you because of your age are likely candidates.

• **Your belief about yourself is important.** To get sex with younger women, you must convince yourself that your age is a benefit. If you go into an interaction with a younger woman trying to pretend you are not older, or acting as if you are doing something wrong, you'll strike out in no time.

• **Young women are more likely to be rude.** Get ready. Younger women are more likely to not show up than are older women. They are more likely to be thoughtless, and to say or do thoughtless things. Therefore, you must always have a back-up plan. They are also more likely to be spacey, or to flip out. Unreliable would be the best word to describe these women. Bring a book to read as you wait for her to show up.

• **Play on your strengths.** Don't try to be 'hip' and 'mod' in a weak attempt to be just like the younger guys. Remember, if she's consenting to date you, it's because you are different. Trying to be hip and modern only makes you look weird. Be interested in modern stuff, and say you like her music or styles if you really do, but don't bother with the Caesar haircut, the cool-again bell bottoms, or putting your cap on backwards. That's not what she'll be looking for from you, anyway.

• **Don't lecture her about age-related stuff.** On the other hand, it's important that you don't give her fatherly advice, and that you never say anything that starts with, "when I was your age…" Your purpose is to seduce her, not to give her guidance about life that she really doesn't want and won't use. Keep focused on the goal—sex.

- **Give her experiences.** You may have the ability to take her someplace her campus-bound peers can't get to, even if it's a walk out of town, or a ride to a romantic restaurant she would never be able to afford but might really like to go to. We're not saying you should lavish her with gifts or blow all your money on her—that would be stupid, and wouldn't be self-respecting. But if you can afford it, put in the extra bucks to make her experiences with you special.

- **Take the time to let it build.** A younger woman needs time to learn to trust you, just as an older woman does. Be willing to go at her pace. That said, when a younger woman decides that she wants you, she'll want to move quickly, and she may decide she wants you so fast that you'll be surprised. Be ready.

Younger women have been in demand by older men since the start of time. You are joining a long, possibly proud tradition. Enjoy it!

36. Only Answer Questions

S ome men feel that they have to explain themselves. Explain, explain, explain. A self-explaining man has a problem. He can never be okay with himself if he thinks that the woman he is with has any kind of problem with him at all. So he is always trying to make her feel at ease by apologizing, explaining himself, and looking for anything about himself that she might find hard to be with. When he finds such a thing he apologizes, explains himself, and hopes that makes things better.

The problem is, this doesn't work. Once again, we tell you: few women are interested in having hot, horny sex with men who approach them as submissive, apologizing little supplicants. They may think you are sweet, or a good conversationalist, and they may take your gifts and compliments and money, but they won't want to have sex with you. Trying to put a woman at ease by explaining why everything about you shouldn't be scary or intimidating or offensive will only put her off. You only have to answer questions—you don't have to answer for everything about yourself that might conceivably discomfort her.

Disobey this rule and you will wreck your seduction in two different ways:

• **You'll explain things you are afraid will scare or annoy her.** This kind of mistake is fatal. A woman we know who is a motivational speaker told us about this one: A man in one of her seminars was very interested in her, so he waited by the door after her presentation 'til everyone had left, so he could talk to her. This would have been fine, but he stupidly felt the need to explain his reason for being there after everyone else had left. He thought that his presence might seem odd. Not realizing he should only answer questions, he took it upon himself to answer her unasked question, "Does your waiting for me mean you are a danger to me?" His first words to her were this: "I'm not stalking you or anything! I just wanted to say hi." This "answer" to a question she didn't even ask did not make our female friend feel better. She told us, "My first thought was, what kind of a guy would have to tell me he's not a stalker? Might he really be one?" By explaining himself unnecessarily, he caused her to think of him as a danger, all in the first 5 seconds of their interaction!

Women take their cues about how dangerous you are from how much concern you have that you are a danger. If you act like you might be a danger to her—and explain yourself accordingly, as this idiot did—then they naturally think you must be a danger. Otherwise, why would you have to answer the "are you a danger?" question before she even thought to ask it? When you are confident, and only answer questions, your belief that you are not a danger to her will be reflected through your behavior. When you explain yourself, your fear that you really might be a danger gets expressed to her instead.

• **You'll explain yourself too much in a conflict.** Men in conflict with women often feel that they have to explain themselves. If a woman asks you a direct question, then answer it, but know this: communication is rarely served by answering questions that she didn't actually ask. Most of the time, answering a question she didn't ask will only make you look defensive, and give her even more ammo to be upset with you about. When you are in a conflict of any magnitude with a woman, stop trying to defend yourself by answering questions she hasn't asked—most of the time she doesn't care to hear about it, anyway. What she wants is for you to *get* what she has to say. She wants to feel heard. And she doesn't feel heard when you are defending yourself from irrelevant questions she hasn't even asked. See the rule "Listen at her" for tips on how to make a woman feel "heard." That's all she really wants anyway.

Only answer questions and you'll be miles ahead of the pack.

37. NEVER STOP LEARNING ABOUT SEDUCTION

Does Michael Jordan (or any other pro athlete) sit on his ass during the off-season feeling good about his accomplishments, thinking that pride alone will be enough to keep him at the top of his game? Does a weightlifter build up his body and then suddenly stop, thinking all the muscle will remain just by sitting in front of a computer screen all day long? You should be saying, NO. Even the best keep working, growing, and learning. And so must you.

This book is teaching you the most cutting edge skills, philosophy, attitudes, and tools available to men today. We have done over four years of research and development, hundreds of interviews, and worked with men of all ages. With that said, what will keep the edge of your blade sharp is to always seeking out new resources, courses, books, mentors, videos, or learning experiences. Most men need to practice these skills over a long period of time for permanent change. Even when change does occur, it takes practice to keep it in place.

A master seducer is always focused on the next level, the next plateau of success with women. *The enemy of true mastery is stagnation.* Whether your goal is more sex, more women, or keeping a long term relationship hot, never relenting in your learning is the only way to get there.

We recommend you contact us for one-on-one training sessions, purchase our upcoming books and tape series', attend our seminars, and keep learning. Also learn from other seduction masters. We have a list of our upcoming products and recommended titles available for your use. Contact us at The Rules, P.O. Box 55094, Madison, WI 53705. Or email us at therules@pobox.com with your questions and concerns about dating. Also let us know about any dating topics you'd like to see materials about.

CONCLUSION

s you follow the Rules, you'll have success with women, and a whole lot more. If you make a practice of following the Rules, they will create in you the character of a "man's man."

A "man's man":

- Expresses himself and his style fully.

- Is unashamed of himself or his sexual desire.

- Creates his life to get what he wants.

- Is not apologetic for who he is, or for any part of him.

- Ackowledges fears and goes on.

- Is able to be compassionate and generous without diminishing his strength.

- Has goals for his life, and is able to produce results.

- Has exactly the relationships with women he wants.

- Has exactly the sex life he wants.

- Is loved and respected for who he is.

- Is able to be both tough and loving, fierce and gentle.

- Doesn't take the events of life personally.

- Is outrageous, playful and is fun to be around.

- Maintains his self respect in every situation.

- Trusts himself.

Follow the rules, and these characteristics will become yours. Go for it, kick ass, and take numbers!

RULES AT A GLANCE:

1) Make her feel special, and she'll give you sex
2) Show your romantic interest right away
3) Rejection is the key to sexual prosperity
4) Don't share everything about yourself
5) Initiate, initiate, initiate
6) It's your job to pursue sex; she has the final say
7) Listen at her
8) Practice where your ego isn't on the line
9) Never expect a woman to call you back
10) Always be prospecting
11) Tips on asking for her phone number and getting the date
12) Always pursue more than one woman
13) Always be willing to walk
14) have a "piece on the side"
15) Get one nut off first
16) Never grovel for sex
17) Be sexually imaginative
18) Don't be her therapist, confidant, or buddy
19) Manage your hygiene

20) Use condoms

21) Watch your back

22) Cut your losses/break up quickly

23) Control all variables

24) Tips on asking for the date

25) Kissing her for the first time

26) For long-term relationships: sacrifice

27) For long-term relationships: always and forever find new ways to delight her

28) Always act with an outcome in mind

29) Avoid fighting with a woman

30) Have personal style

31) Never hit a woman

32) Blow off steam away from her

33) Make it look like you are not working

34) Make it work for you

35) Don't expect a woman to have integrity the same way you do

36) Rules for handling women younger than you

37) Only answer questions

38) Never stop learning about seduction
